Dedication

This love poem is dedicated to all women and girls everywhere…whether living on the streets or in a penthouse apartment…whether working in a sweatshop or in a corner office in a high-rise office building…who have ever been mistreated…under attack…because they are female.

All profits from the sale of this book are being donated to shelters for women, girls, and families.

Gender inequality, manifest in its most destructive forms as emotional, mental, physical, and sexual abuse of women and girls, has become so entrenched in human society today as to seem almost intractable.

And yet there is comfort to be found in reminding ourselves that at all times a new earth is being born through us. Just as the joy of holding our newborn for the first time more than eclipses the pain of childbirth, so the joy of living freely and safely in a world shaped by gender equality will someday eclipse the agony of living in–and fighting to change–a world now horribly misshapen by inequalities and violence against women and girls.

In the meantime, may this poem remind each of us, whether we are directly or indirectly affected by violence against women and girls, that we are never alone. Each of us is loved beyond our capacity to imagine. Each of us is redeemed.

For

My Grandmothers, Alice and Minnie

My Mother, Adele

My Daughter, Adira

My Sister, Cheryl

And All of my Spirit Mothers and Sisters

I AM!!!

Written by Deidra Roach-Quarles
Illustrated by Sherri Roberts Lumpkin

Copyright © 2016 by Sepia Works LLC. All Rights Reserved.

Cover design and formatting by Nabeeh Bilal

This book or any portion thereof may not be reproduced or used in any manner whatsoever without the express written permission of the publisher except for the use of brief quotations in a book review.

I AM!
I AM!!
I AM!!!

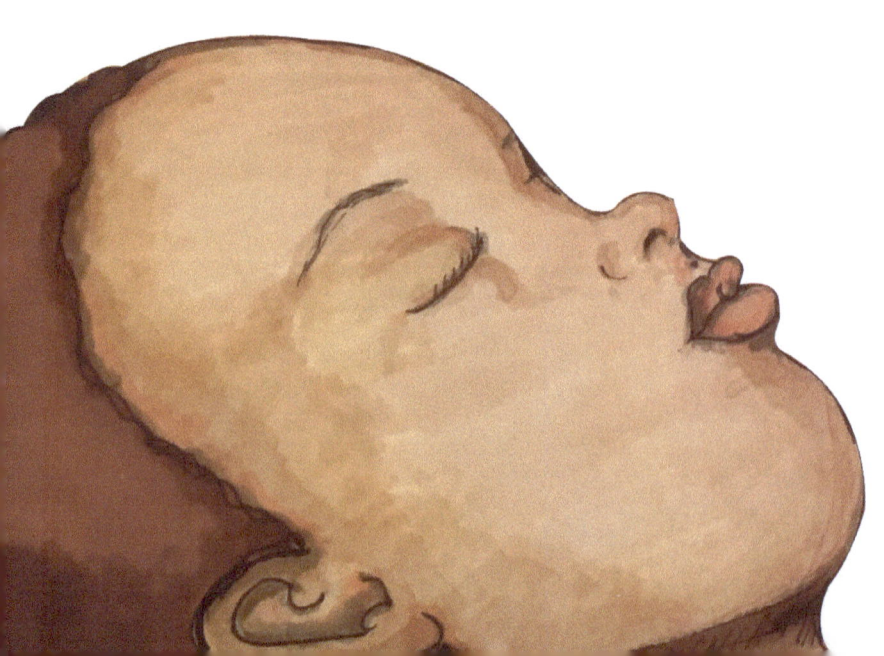

Compassionate and kind!!!
More compassion mine than ebon angel
Who bending low to dying child
Heals all her hurt and hungry places
And pulls from pain a cherub's smile
That's how kind

I AM!!!

I AM healthy and whole!

More whole, complete, and vast am I
Than midnight Kalahari sky
Enfolding moon and galaxy
In equal measure tenderly
Indivisible by jealous thought or blade
Who bends her nubile breast to Earth
And swaddles Her in deep nightshade
Inviting sweet and sacred rest
That's how whole
How complete

I AM!!!

I AM Brilliant!

More brilliance mine than a thousand diamonds
Blazing in the mind of Ya
More passion mine than fires burning
In wildly flaming tongues of Ra
My kiss upon the cheek of Earth
So searing that it bakes
My kiss upon your quaking mouth
So fevered that it aches
With all-consuming kiss I scorch you
Past remembrance of the lie
The rank, decaying, breath-betraying
Grimly gold sarcophagi in which you sadly
So madly lose yourselves
Until the thrill of Light
That's how brilliant

I AM!!!

I AM Rich!

More wealth have I than Tutankhamun
More worth than Mansa Musa's gold
More bounty mine than Nubian gardens'
Impassioned fruit made manifold
That's how rich

I AM!!!

I AM Free!

More freedom mine than would-be slave
Who breaks the bite of bone-gnawing shackle
To breach the crush of Neptune's grave
To dance with wind and sing with thunder
To skip upon the moonstruck wave
That's how free

I AM!!!

I AM Beautiful!
More beauty mine than Nefertiti's
Sable eyes inlaid with stars
Her voice a prayer sung by lutes
Of God-besotted avatars

Aten wakes
Dawn breaks
From the Queen's pearlescent smile
Her lips a rubricate ambrosia
Her cheek a Lily of the Nile

Beauty you cannot resist
Who sucks you into her tempest eye
Drops you screaming through God's Window
Hurls you through her flaming sky

Beauty that tears through all defenses
Beauty that swallows body, soul
Burps you up in a sea of rapture
Shatters you and makes you whole

And, Oh
You are so glad for it!

That's how beautiful

I AM!!!

I AM a giver of Life!

More creative am I
Than First Lover of Eden
More fertile am I
Than first Mother of Man
Right foot plunged in roiling ocean
Left foot plunged in raging sand

My hips astride the Oldevai yearning
My flower open to receive
Sweet nectar of Love's pure devotion
Sweet ecstasy of primal Eve

Life rushes to Me
Life gushes through Me
In surging rivers
Pulsing streams
Sewing seeds of teeming nations
Planting roots of primal dreams
I scream
Into the pregnant silence
Worlds fall down around My feet
As I rise to My own healing
Where My Love is made complete

My trembling flesh now baptized
In the sanctity of "YES!!!"
Arid wastelands quenched to bursting
Thirsting flowers effloresced
That's how fertile

I AM!!!

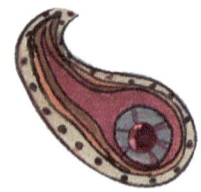 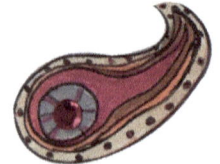

I AM Powerful!

Beyond your deepest imagination

Strong!!!
Beyond your deepest fears

Ten thousand armies formed against me
Live to drown in their own tears
While I
While I
While I
After 10,000 bomb-bashed
War-slashed years
Am still
Standing
Here

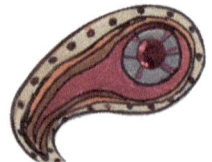 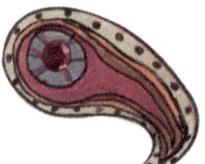

Beaten

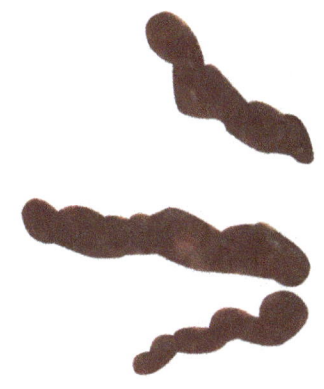

Raped

Bleeding

Maimed

Mutilated

And yet
Still standing
Here

Still
Compassionate!!!

Still
Kind!!!

Still
Healthy!!!

Still
Whole!!!

Still
Brilliant!!!

Still
Free!!!

Still
Beautiful!!!

Still
Fertile!!!

Still
Powerful!!!

Still
Strong!!!

Beyond
Your deepest imagination

Beyond
Your darkest fears

Still
Giving new life
To your every
Dying breath

You can never undermine
My knowledge of who
I AM!!!

For
I AM!!!
Knowledge Itself!!!

I AM!!!
Wisdom Itself!!!

I AM!!!
Understanding Itself!!!

I AM!!!
Love Itself!!!

I AM!!!
Always becoming!!!

I AM!!!
Simply
Beyond words!!!

There are no words vast enough
To contain who

I AM!!!

But…
If you insist upon taking my name
And trying to circumscribe my number
Know that

I AM!!!

An altogether

FABULOUS!!!

UNSTOPPABLE!!!

UNBREAKABLE!!!

From my FAITH, my LOVE
UNSHAKABLE!!!

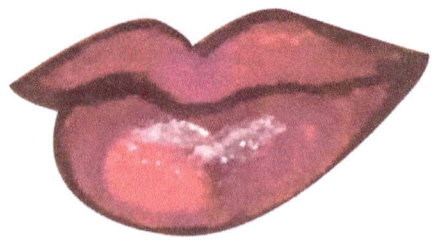

DAUGHTER OF GOD!!!

I AM!
I AM!!
I AM!!!

Thank GOD Almighty!!!

AMEN!!!

www.ingramcontent.com/pod-product-compliance
Lightning Source LLC
Chambersburg PA
CBHW040555010526
44110CB00055B/2814